THE HAPPY

(happy!!!)

HOLIDAY

POT COOKIE

COOKBOOK

———

DR. SEYMOUR
KINDBUD

13-Digit ISBN: 978-1-60433-830-0
10-Digit ISBN: 1-60433-830-X

This book may only be ordered as part of the *Happy (Happy!!!) Holiday Pot Cookie Cookbook Kit*
(13-Digit ISBN: 978-1-60433-827-0; 10-Digit ISBN: 1-60433-827-X). The kit can be
ordered by mail from the publisher. Please include $5.99 for postage and handling.
Please support your local bookseller first!

Books published by Cider Mill Press Book Publishers are available at special discounts for
bulk purchases in the United States by corporations, institutions, and other organizations.
For more information, please contact the publisher.

Cider Mill Press Book Publishers
"Where good books are ready for press"
PO Box 454
12 Spring Street
Kennebunkport, Maine 04046
Visit us online! www.cidermillpress.com

Typography: Mrs Eaves, Academy Engraved, Chopin Script

Printed in China
1 2 3 4 5 6 7 8 9 0
First Edition

TABLE OF CONTENTS

INTRODUCTION

When Alice B. Toklas, the Julia Child of ganja, started adding hash to her brownies she probably never envisioned there being a whole book devoted to celebrating the holidays by chewing some cheeba.

But that's exactly what *The Happy (Happy!!!) Holiday Pot Cookie Cookbook* is all about. You'll get to enjoy the holiday flavors you've grown to love, all while getting high. Right here is a game plan to ensure that you and your friends can get lit up like a Christmas tree without ever lighting up.

While this book guarantees that your holidays are filled with sugar, spice, and everything nice, it also intends to improve your high. When eaten, the tetrahydrocannabinol (THC) that makes marijuana so lovely is transformed into a powerful compound by the liver. The high takes a little longer to kick in, but it can also last for up to five hours, meaning that the gifts in this book just keep on giving.

You may think you're no Betty Crocker. You may think baking is hard. But if I can make these cookies and candies, anyone can. Trust me, you don't want to let all these tasty treats go by. Cannabis and Christmas, together at last. Does it get any better?

BAKING BASICS

Ganja Butter

Ganja Butter is the mother's milk of cannabis cookies and candies. The THC in the weed is transferred to the fat in the butter, and the water in which it's all boiling keeps it from scorching.

Making Ganja Butter is more of a method and a formula than a recipe, and you can do a few pounds of butter at a time; it keeps for a few weeks in the refrigerator, and can last for up to six months if frozen. But it never lasts that long in my house! And it certainly won't last that long when making cookies either.

The formulation is 1 stick of unsalted butter (¼ pound) per ¼ to ½ ounce of weed. This particular recipe is for up to 1 pound of Ganja Butter; if you're interested in scaling it up to this amount, make sure you add more water to the pan.

1 STICK UNSALTED BUTTER

¼ TO ½ OZ. MARIJUANA

2 CUPS WATER

1. Bring the water to boil in a saucepan. Grind the marijuana in a grinder or with a mortar and pestle. Add the butter to the saucepan. When it is melted, stir in the ground marijuana and reduce the heat to low. Cover the pan and simmer for 2 hours, stirring occasionally.

2. Strain the liquid into a bowl through a fine sieve lined with a few layers of cheesecloth or a few coffee filters. Let the liquid sit at room temperature until cool, cover it with plastic wrap, and refrigerate it overnight, or until the butter on top of the liquid has formed a solid layer. Pull off the solid stuff and throw out the liquid stuff. *Voila!* You've got a stash of Ganja Butter.

Careful Creaming

Perhaps the most vital step in the creation of cookie dough is the "creaming" of the butter and sugar. During this process, air is trapped in the butter's crystalline structure. It is the number and size of the air bubbles (which then become enlarged by the carbon dioxide produced by baking soda or baking powder) that leavens a dough or batter to produce a finely textured product.

The starting point in proper creaming is to ensure that the butter is at the correct temperature, approximately 70° F. To do this, remove your Ganja Butter from the refrigerator and cut it into small pieces. Allow them to sit at room temperature for 15 to 20 minutes to soften.

When the pieces have softened, place them in the bowl of your electric mixer and beat until they have broken into even smaller pieces. Add the sugar, and beat at medium speed to start the process of combining them. Then increase the speed to high, and scrape the bowl frequently. When properly creamed the texture of the butter and sugar mixture will be light and fluffy.

Creating a Cookie Dough Cache

Cookie doughs are not only easy to make, they're just about indestructible. You can successfully freeze cookie dough and bake off individual cookies or a whole batch at a moment's notice, such as when your friends decide to drop by unexpectedly.

If you want to freeze a whole batch of dough, do so in a heavy, resealable plastic bag and allow it to thaw overnight in the refrigerator. But I find it's much easier to freeze individual balls of dough.

To do this, cover a baking sheet with plastic wrap and form the dough into balls. Place the balls on the cookie sheet (you can place them close together because they're not going to spread). Place the balls in the freezer and, once they are frozen solid, transfer to a heavy, resealable plastic bag. When you want to whip up a couple of treats, it's not necessary to thaw the frozen dough balls. Just add 2 to 3 minutes to the baking time.

RECIPES

BONKERS GINGERBREAD COOKIES

¾ CUP GANJA BUTTER (SEE RECIPE ON PAGE 8), SOFTENED

½ CUP LIGHT BROWN SUGAR, FIRMLY PACKED

⅔ CUP UNSULFURED MOLASSES

1 LARGE EGG AT ROOM TEMPERATURE

1 TEASPOON BAKING SODA

1 TEASPOON GROUND GINGER

1 TEASPOON APPLE PIE SPICE

½ TEASPOON SALT

½ TEASPOON PURE VANILLA EXTRACT

¼ TEASPOON FRESHLY GROUND BLACK PEPPER

3 CUPS ALL-PURPOSE FLOUR

ROYAL ICING OR CONFECTIONERS' SUGAR GLAZE (RECIPES TO FOLLOW)

ASSORTED SMALL CANDIES FOR DECORATION, OPTIONAL

1. Place the butter and brown sugar in a mixing bowl, and beat at low speed with an electric mixer until combined. Increase the speed to high, and beat for 3 to 4 minutes, or until the mixture is light and fluffy. Add molasses, egg, baking soda, ginger, apple pie spice, salt, vanilla, and pepper, and beat for 1 minute. Slowly add flour to the mixture and beat until stiff dough forms.

2. Divide dough in half and wrap each half in plastic wrap. Press dough into a pancake. Refrigerate dough for at least 1 hour and up to 2 days.

3. Preheat the oven to 350° F. Line two baking sheets and lightly dust a sheet of waxed paper and a rolling pin with flour. Roll dough to a thickness of ⅛ inch. Dip cookie cutters in flour, and cut cookies into desired shapes. Set excess dough aside and transfer cookies to the baking sheets. Roll the excess dough again, chilling it for 15 minutes if necessary.

4. Bake cookies for 10 to 12 minutes, or until firm. Remove cookies from oven, let rest on the sheets for 2 minutes, and then set on wire racks to cool completely. Decorate with Royal Icing or Confectioners' Sugar Glaze, and candies, if using.

CONFECTIONERS' SUGAR GLAZE

This recipe will yield 1 ½ cups, and is the most basic way to decorate your cookies.

4 CUPS CONFECTIONERS' SUGAR

4 TO 5 TABLESPOONS WATER

½ TEASPOON CLEAR VANILLA EXTRACT

FOOD COLORING (OPTIONAL)

1. Combine the confectioners' sugar, 4 tablespoons water, and vanilla in a mixing bowl. Stir until the mixture is smooth, adding additional water if it is too thick.

2. If you want to color your glaze, transfer it to small cups and add the food coloring a few drops at a time until the desired color is reached. Stir well before adding additional coloring.

ROYAL ICING

This frosting can only be used on cookies that are kept at room temperature. Refrigerating the cookies can cause the frosting to become overly sticky. This recipe will provide you with 3 ½ cups of icing.

3 LARGE EGG WHITES AT ROOM TEMPERATURE

½ TEASPOON CREAM OF TARTAR

¼ TEASPOON SALT

4 CUPS CONFECTIONERS' SUGAR

½ TEASPOON PURE VANILLA EXTRACT

FOOD COLORING (OPTIONAL)

1. Place the egg whites in a mixing bowl and beat at medium speed with an electric mixer until frothy. Add the cream of tartar and salt, raise the speed to high, and beat until soft peaks form.

2. Add the sugar and beat at low speed. Raise the speed to high and beat for 5 to 7 minutes, until mixture is glossy and stiff peaks form. Beat in the vanilla.

3. If tinting icing, transfer it to small cups and add food coloring, a few drops at a time, until desired color is reached. Stir well before adding additional coloring.

REEFER ROLLED-OUT SUGAR COOKIES

¾ CUP GANJA BUTTER
(SEE RECIPE ON PAGE 8)

¾ CUP GRANULATED SUGAR

1 LARGE EGG AT
ROOM TEMPERATURE

1 TEASPOON PURE
VANILLA EXTRACT

½ TEASPOON SALT

2½ CUPS ALL-PURPOSE FLOUR

ROYAL ICING (SEE RECIPE ON
PAGE 14); (OPTIONAL)

CONFECTIONERS' SUGAR
GLAZE (SEE RECIPE ON PAGE 13);
(OPTIONAL)

ASSORTED SMALL CANDIES FOR
DECORATION (OPTIONAL)

1. Place the butter and sugar in a mixing bowl, and beat at low speed with an electric mixer until combined. Increase the speed to high, and beat for 3 to 4 minutes, or until the mixture is light and fluffy. Add egg, vanilla, and salt, and beat for 1 minute. Slowly add flour to the mixture, and beat until stiff dough forms.

2. Divide dough in half and wrap each half in plastic wrap. Press dough into a pancake. Refrigerate dough for at least 1 hour and up to 2 days.

3. Preheat the oven to 350° F. Line two baking sheets and lightly dust a sheet of waxed paper and a rolling pin with flour. Roll dough to a thickness of ¼ inch. Dip cookie cutters in flour, and cut cookies into desired shapes. Set excess dough aside and transfer cookies to the baking sheets. Re-roll excess dough, chilling it for 15 minutes if necessary.

4. Bake cookies for 10 to 12 minutes, until the edges are brown. Remove cookies from the oven, let rest on baking sheets for 2 minutes, and then set on wire racks to cool completely. Decorate with Royal Icing, Confectioners' Sugar Glaze, and candies, if desired.

PSYCHEDELIC STAINED GLASS COOKIES

1 CUP GANJA BUTTER
(SEE RECIPE ON PAGE 8)

¾ CUP GRANULATED SUGAR

½ CUP LIGHT BROWN SUGAR,
FIRMLY PACKED

1 LARGE EGG AT
ROOM TEMPERATURE

½ TEASPOON RUM EXTRACT

½ TEASPOON SALT

3¼ CUPS ALL-PURPOSE FLOUR

1 (7 OZ.) PACKAGE OF BRIGHTLY
COLORED HARD CANDY (SUCH
AS SOUR BALLS)

1. Place the butter, granulated sugar, and brown sugar in a mixing bowl and beat at low speed with an electric mixer until combined. Increase the speed to high, and beat for 3 to 4 minutes, or until the mixture is light and fluffy. Add egg, rum extract, and salt, and beat for 1 minute. Slowly add flour to the mixture, and beat until stiff dough forms.

2. Divide dough in half and wrap each half in plastic wrap. Press dough into a pancake. Refrigerate dough for at least 1 hour and up to 2 days.

3. While the dough chills, divide the candies into groupings by color in separate heavy-duty plastic bags. Pound candies with the bottom of a small saucepan until crushed. Preheat the oven to 350° F. Line two baking sheets with parchment paper or silicon baking mats.

4. Lightly dust a sheet of waxed paper and a rolling pin with flour. Roll dough to a thickness of ¼ inch. Dip cookie cutters in flour, cut cookies into desired shapes, and set excess dough aside. Roll the excess dough again, chilling it for 15 minutes if necessary. Use smaller cutters to create designs inside of larger cookies, fill holes with crushed candy, and transfer cookies to the baking sheets. Bake cookies for 10 to 12 minutes, or until the edges are brown. Remove the cookies from the oven, let rest on baking sheets for 2 minutes, and then set on wire racks to cool completely.

WACKY WEED
CORNMEAL COOKIES

½ CUP GANJA BUTTER
(SEE RECIPE ON PAGE 8)

¾ CUP CONFECTIONERS' SUGAR

1 LARGE EGG AT
ROOM TEMPERATURE

½ TEASPOON VANILLA EXTRACT

⅔ CUP ALL-PURPOSE FLOUR

¼ CUP FINELY
GROUND CORNMEAL

2 TABLESPOONS CORNSTARCH

¼ TEASPOON SALT

COLORED SUGARS

1. Combine the butter and confectioners' sugar in a mixing bowl and beat at low speed with an electric mixer. Increase the speed to high and beat for 3 to 4 minutes, until light and fluffy. Add the egg and vanilla, beat for 1 minute, and then slowly add the flour, cornmeal, cornstarch, and salt. Beat until a stiff dough forms.

2. Place the dough on a sheet of waxed paper and form it into a log 2½ inches in diameter. Cover in plastic wrap and refrigerate for at least 2 hours and up to 2 days.

3. Preheat the oven to 350° F. Line two baking sheets and cut chilled dough into ⅓-inch thick slices using a sharp serrated knife. Arrange the cookies on the baking sheets and decorate with colored sugars. Place the cookies in the oven and bake for 10 to 12 minutes, until the edges are brown. Remove, let cool on sheets for 2 minutes, and then transfer the cookies to wire racks to cool completely.

LOCO WEED LEMON COCONUT SANDWICH COOKIES

Cookies

1 CUP UNSWEETENED
SHREDDED COCONUT

1 CUP GANJA BUTTER (SEE RECIPE
ON PAGE 8), SOFTENED

⅓ CUP GRANULATED SUGAR

1 TABLESPOON LEMON ZEST,
GRATED

1 TEASPOON LEMON OIL

2 CUPS ALL-PURPOSE FLOUR

½ TEASPOON SALT

COLORED SUGARS (OPTIONAL)

Filling

1 CUP CONFECTIONERS' SUGAR

¼ CUP GANJA BUTTER

1 TABLESPOON LEMON ZEST

1 TABLESPOON FRESHLY
SQUEEZED LEMON JUICE

2 TABLESPOONS
LIGHT CORN SYRUP

1. Preheat the oven to 325° F. Place the coconut flakes on a baking sheet and toast for 10 to 12 minutes, while stirring occasionally. When flakes are lightly browned, remove from oven and set aside.

2. Combine the butter, sugar, lemon zest, and lemon oil in a mixing bowl and beat at low speed with an electric mixer to blend. Increase the speed to high and beat for 3 to 4 minutes, until light and fluffy. Slowly add the flour and salt and beat until a soft dough forms. Add the toasted coconut and beat until combined.

3. Place the dough on a sheet of waxed paper and form it into a log 2½ inches in diameter. Cover in plastic wrap and refrigerate for at least 2 hours and up to 2 days.

4. Preheat the oven to 350° F. Line two baking sheets and then cut the chilled dough into ¼-inch thick slices. Arrange cookies on the baking sheets and decorate with colored sugars, if using. Place the cookies in the oven and cook for 10 to 12 minutes, until the edges are brown. Remove baking sheets, allow cookies to cool for 2 minutes, and then transfer the cookies to wire racks to cool completely.

5. Prepare the filling. Combine the confectioners' sugar, butter, lemon zest, lemon juice, and corn syrup in a bowl and beat at low speed with an electric mixer. When combined, increase the speed and beat until mixture is light and fluffy. Place 1 teaspoon of filling on the flat side of a cookie and top with the flat side of another cookie. Repeat until all of the cookies have been used and then place in refrigerator for 15 minutes.

MINTY GRASSHOPPER SANDWICH COOKIES

Cookies

1 CUP GANJA BUTTER (SEE RECIPE ON PAGE 8), SOFTENED

¼ CUP GRANULATED SUGAR

1 LARGE EGG YOLK AT ROOM TEMPERATURE

½ TEASPOON PURE VANILLA EXTRACT

½ TEASPOON BAKING POWDER

½ TEASPOON SALT

½ CUP UNSWEETENED COCOA POWDER

2 CUPS ALL-PURPOSE FLOUR

Filling

½ CUP HEAVY CREAM

1½ TABLESPOONS LIGHT CORN SYRUP

¾ POUND QUALITY WHITE CHOCOLATE, DICED

2 TABLESPOONS GANJA BUTTER

1 TEASPOON MINT OIL OR EXTRACT

¼ TEASPOON RED OR GREEN FOOD COLORING (OPTIONAL)

CONFECTIONERS' SUGAR GLAZE (SEE RECIPE ON PAGE 13); (OPTIONAL)

1. Combine the butter and sugar in a mixing bowl and beat at low speed with an electric mixer to blend. Increase the speed to high and beat for 3 to 4 minutes, until light and fluffy. Add the egg yolk, vanilla, baking powder, and salt and beat for 1 minute. Slowly add cocoa powder and flour to butter mixture and beat until a stiff dough forms.

2. Place the dough on a sheet of waxed paper and form it into a log 2½ inches in diameter. Cover in plastic wrap and refrigerate for at least 2 hours and up to 2 days.

3. Prepare the filling. Place the cream and corn syrup in a small saucepan and bring to a simmer. Stir in the white chocolate, butter, and mint component, cover the pan, and remove from heat. Allow mixture to sit for 5 minutes. Stir well and, if using, stir in food coloring. Heat over very low heat if chocolate still has lumps. Press a sheet of waxed paper onto the surface and refrigerate.

4. Preheat the oven to 350° F. Line two baking sheets and cut the chilled dough into ½-inch thick slices. Arrange them on the baking sheets, place in the oven, and bake for 10 to 12 minutes, until the edges are brown. Remove from oven, cool on baking sheets for 2 minutes, and then place on a wire rack to cool completely.

5. Beat filling with an electric mixer on medium speed until it is light and fluffy. Place a dollop on the flat side of 1 cookie and top with the flat side of another cookie. Decorate cookies with Confectioners' Sugar Glaze, if desired. Repeat until all the cookies have been used.

CHOCOLATE CANDY REEFER REFRIGERATOR COOKIES

¾ CUP GANJA BUTTER (SEE RECIPE ON PAGE 8), SOFTENED

½ CUP GRANULATED SUGAR

¾ TEASPOON VANILLA EXTRACT

2 LARGE EGG YOLKS AT ROOM TEMPERATURE

1¾ CUPS ALL-PURPOSE FLOUR

1½ CUPS MINIATURE CHOCOLATE CHIPS

1. Combine the butter, sugar, and vanilla in a mixing bowl and beat at medium speed with an electric mixer to blend. Increase the speed to high and beat until the mixture is light and fluffy. Reduce the speed to medium, add the egg yolks, and beat well, scraping the sides of the bowl as necessary. Reduce the speed to low, add the flour, and combine.

2. Scrape the dough onto a floured surface and divide it in half. Roll each piece into a log 2 inches in diameter. Cover in plastic wrap and refrigerate for at least 2 hours and up to 2 days.

3. Preheat the oven to 350° F. Grease or line two baking sheets and then cut the chilled dough into ⅓-inch thick slices. Place cookies 1 inch apart on the baking sheets and pat the chocolate chips down on top. Place the cookies in the oven and cook for 12 to 15 minutes, until the edges are lightly brown. Remove baking sheets and transfer the cookies to wire racks to cool completely.

ATOMIC ALL ABOUT ALMOND BARS

1¼ CUPS ALL-PURPOSE FLOUR

¾ CUP CONFECTIONERS' SUGAR

½ TEASPOON BAKING SODA

¼ TEASPOON SALT

¾ CUP GANJA BUTTER
(SEE RECIPE ON PAGE 8)

⅔ CUP ALMOND PASTE

1 LARGE EGG AT
ROOM TEMPERATURE

1 TABLESPOON WHOLE MILK

1 TEASPOON ALMOND EXTRACT

1 LARGE EGG WHITE

1 CUP SLICED ALMONDS

1. Preheat the oven to 350° F. Grease a 9 x 9-inch baking pan.

2. Combine flour, confectioners' sugar, baking soda, and salt in a food processor and blend for 5 seconds. Add the butter and almond paste and blend until the mixture resembles coarse meal.

3. Combine the egg, milk, and almond extract in a small cup and whisk until well combined. Drizzle liquid into the work bowl of the food processor and pulse about 10 times, until a stiff dough forms. If dough is dry, add milk in 1-teaspoon increments until dough forms a ball.

4. Press the dough into the prepared pan. Whisk the egg white in a small cup and spread over the dough. Distribute sliced almonds evenly and pat them into the dough. Place the baking dish in the oven and bake for 35 to 40 minutes, until the top is golden. Remove from oven, allow to cool completely in the pan, and then cut into bars.

CARAMEL PECAN BAMBA BARS

Bars

1 CUP ALL-PURPOSE FLOUR

⅓ CUP CONFECTIONERS' SUGAR

¼ TEASPOON SALT

½ CUP GANJA BUTTER
(SEE RECIPE ON PAGE 8)

1 LARGE EGG AT
ROOM TEMPERATURE

½ TEASPOON PURE
VANILLA EXTRACT

¼ TEASPOON PURE
ALMOND EXTRACT

Topping

½ POUND PECAN HALVES

¾ CUP LIGHT BROWN SUGAR,
FIRMLY PACKED

¼ CUP LIGHT CORN SYRUP

¼ CUP HEAVY CREAM

---

1. Preheat the oven to 375° F. Line a 9 x 9-inch baking pan with heavy duty aluminum foil and grease the foil. Place pecans on a baking sheet and toast for 5 to 7 minutes, or until lightly browned. Set aside until it is time to prepare the topping.

2. Combine flour, confectioners' sugar, and salt in a food processor and blend for 5 seconds. Add the butter and pulse until mixture resembles coarse meal.

3. Combine egg, vanilla, and almond extract in a small cup, and whisk well. Drizzle liquid into the work bowl of the food processor, and pulse about 10 times, or until a stiff dough forms. If dough is dry and won't come together, add milk in 1-teaspoon increments until the dough forms a ball.

4. Transfer dough to the prepared baking pan. Using flour-covered fingers and an offset spatula, press dough firmly into the bottom of the pan and ¾ inch up the sides. Freeze until firm, about 15 minutes. Remove and prick the dough on the bottom of the pan with the tines of a fork. Bake crust for 10 to 12 minutes, or until lightly browned.

5. While crust bakes, prepare the topping. Combine the butter, brown sugar, and corn syrup in a saucepan, and bring to a boil over high heat, whisking constantly. Boil for 2 minutes, remove pan from heat, and stir in cream and pecans.

6. Spoon topping over crust, smoothing the top with a spatula. Bake for 20 to 22 minutes, or until the topping is bubbling and dark brown. Remove from the oven and cool completely in the pan. Remove cookies from the pan by pulling up on the sides of the foil and cut into bars.

AUNT MARY'S WHITE CHOCOLATE ALMOND SQUARES

1 CUP ALMONDS, BLANCHED AND CHOPPED

1 CUP GANJA BUTTER (SEE RECIPE ON PAGE 8)

1 CUP DARK BROWN SUGAR, FIRMLY PACKED

1 LARGE EGG YOLK AT ROOM TEMPERATURE

1 TEASPOON VANILLA EXTRACT

2 CUPS ALL-PURPOSE FLOUR

¼ TEASPOON SALT

½ POUND QUALITY WHITE CHOCOLATE, CHOPPED

1. Preheat the oven to 350° F. Line a 9 x 13-inch baking pan with parchment paper. Place almonds on a baking sheet and toast for 5 to 7 minutes, until lightly browned. Set almonds aside.

2. Combine the butter and sugar in a mixing bowl and beat at low speed with an electric mixer to blend. Increase the speed to high and beat for 3 to 4 minutes, until light and fluffy. Add the egg yolk and vanilla and beat for 1 minute. Slowly add the flour and salt and beat until a stiff dough forms. Pat the dough evenly into the baking pan and prick it with the tines of a fork. Place the pan on the middle rack in the oven and cook for 20 minutes, or until light brown.

3. Remove the pan from the oven and scatter the chocolate evenly over the crust. Return the pan to the oven for 1 minute, remove, and spread the chocolate into an even layer. Sprinkle the almonds on top, allow to cool in the pan, and then cut into bars.

WHITE CHOCOLATE TWISTED PEPPERMINT SHORTBREADS

1 CUP GANJA BUTTER
(SEE RECIPE ON PAGE 8)

1 CUP GRANULATED SUGAR

1 LARGE EGG AT
ROOM TEMPERATURE

½ TEASPOON PEPPERMINT OIL
OR EXTRACT

½ TEASPOON VANILLA EXTRACT

2 CUPS ALL-PURPOSE FLOUR

¼ TEASPOON SALT

10 OZ. QUALITY WHITE
CHOCOLATE, DICED

¾ CUP RED-AND-WHITE
PEPPERMINTS, CRUSHED

1. Preheat the oven to 350° F. Line a 9 x 13-inch baking pan with heavy-duty aluminum foil and grease the foil.

2. Combine the butter and sugar in a mixing bowl and beat at low speed with an electric mixer to blend. Increase the speed to high and beat for 3 to 4 minutes, until light and fluffy. Add the egg, peppermint component, and vanilla and beat for 1 minute. Slowly add flour and salt and beat until a stiff dough forms. Pat the dough evenly into the baking pan and prick it with the tines of a fork. Place the pan on the middle rack in the oven and cook for 20 to 25 minutes, or until light brown.

4. Remove the pan from the oven and scatter the chocolate evenly over the crust. Return the pan to the oven for 1 minute, remove, and spread the chocolate into an even layer. Sprinkle the crushed peppermints on top, allow to cool in the pan, and then cut into bars.

CHEEBA CHOCOLATE COCONUT BARS

1 CUP GANJA BUTTER
(SEE RECIPE ON PAGE 8)

¾ CUP GRANULATED SUGAR

¾ CUP LIGHT BROWN SUGAR,
FIRMLY PACKED

2 LARGE EGGS AT
ROOM TEMPERATURE

1 TEASPOON PURE
ALMOND EXTRACT

¼ CUP UNSWEETENED
COCOA POWDER

1 TEASPOON BAKING SODA

½ TEASPOON SALT

2 CUPS ALL-PURPOSE FLOUR

1 CUP MINIATURE
CHOCOLATE CHIPS

1 (14 OZ.) CAN SWEETENED
CONDENSED MILK

1 CUP UNSWEETENED COCONUT
FLAKES, FIRMLY PACKED

1. Preheat the oven to 375° F and grease a 9 x 13-inch baking pan. Combine the butter, granulated sugar, and brown sugar in a mixing bowl and beat at low speed with an electric mixer to blend. Increase the speed to high and beat for 3 to 4 minutes, until light and fluffy.

2. Add cocoa powder, baking soda, and salt and beat at medium speed. Reduce the speed to low, add the flour, and then fold in the chocolate chips. Add the eggs and almond extract and beat until well combined.

3. Spread the batter in the pan. Combine the condensed milk and coconut in a small bowl and stir well. Spread this in an even layer on top of the batter. Place the pan in the oven and bake for 25 to 30 minutes, until a toothpick comes out clean after being inserted. Remove from the oven, allow to cool in the pan, and then cut into bars.

LOCO WEED
LEMON SQUARES

½ CUP GANJA BUTTER
(SEE RECIPE ON PAGE 8)

⅓ CUP CONFECTIONERS' SUGAR,

1 CUP ALL-PURPOSE FLOUR,
PLUS 2 TABLESPOONS

PINCH OF SALT

2 LARGE EGGS AT
ROOM TEMPERATURE

1 CUP GRANULATED SUGAR

⅓ CUP FRESHLY SQUEEZED
LEMON JUICE

1 TABLESPOON LEMON ZEST

1. Preheat the oven to 350° F and grease the bottom and sides of an 8 x 8-inch baking pan.

2. Place butter, ¼ cup of the confectioners' sugar, 1 cup flour, and salt in a mixing bowl and stir until combined. Press mixture into the baking pan and bake for 20 minutes, or until it is set and lightly browned. Remove from oven and set aside.

3. Place the eggs, remaining flour, granulated sugar, lemon juice, and lemon zest in a mixing bowl and beat with an electric mixer on medium until well combined. Pour mixture over crust and bake for 20 minutes, or until barely browned. The custard should still be soft. Let the pan cool on a wire rack, then dust with the remaining confectioners' sugar and cut into bars.

VIXEN'S CHOCOLATE PEPPERMINT BROWNIES

3 OZ. BITTERSWEET CHOCOLATE, CHOPPED

¼ CUP HEAVY CREAM

1 CUP ALL-PURPOSE FLOUR

3 TABLESPOONS UNSWEETENED COCOA POWDER

½ TEASPOON SALT

¾ CUP GANJA BUTTER (SEE RECIPE ON PAGE 8), SOFTENED

2½ CUPS CONFECTIONERS' SUGAR

2 LARGE EGGS

½ TEASPOON VANILLA EXTRACT

½ TO 1 TEASPOON MINT OIL

¾ CUP RED-AND-WHITE PEPPERMINTS, CRUSHED

2 TO 4 DROPS RED FOOD COLORING (OPTIONAL)

1. Preheat the oven to 350° F and grease a 9 x 9-inch baking pan. Combine the chocolate and 2 tablespoons of the cream in a microwave-safe bowl and microwave on medium for 30-second intervals until melted and smooth, removing to stir in between each interval.

2. Combine the flour, cocoa powder, and salt in a mixing bowl and whisk until well combined. Combine ½ cup of the butter and ½ cup of the sugar in a mixing bowl and beat at low speed with an electric mixer to blend. Increase the speed to high and beat for 3 to 4 minutes, until light and fluffy. Add the eggs one at a time and beat well between each addition. Add chocolate-and-cream mixture and the vanilla. When combined, slowly add the flour-and-cocoa mixture and beat until a dough forms.

3. Scrape the batter into the prepared pan and spread evenly. Place in the oven and bake for 15 minutes, until the brownies are firm and a toothpick inserted into the center comes out clean. Remove and allow to cool in the pan. While the brownies are cooling, place the remaining butter, sugar, and cream in a mixing bowl and beat at medium speed until light and fluffy. Add the mint oil and, if using, red food coloring and beat until well combined. Add cream in 1-teaspoon increments if frosting is too thick. Spread frosting over cooled brownies, sprinkle the crushed peppermints on top, and cut into small bars.

ALICE B. TOKLAS WHITE CHOCOLATE MARBLE BROWNIES

½ CUP GANJA BUTTER
(SEE RECIPE ON PAGE 8)

4 OZ. WHITE CHOCOLATE,
CHOPPED

3 LARGE EGGS AT
ROOM TEMPERATURE

1 CUP GRANULATED SUGAR

½ CUP ALL-PURPOSE FLOUR

PINCH OF SALT

1 (8 OZ.) PACKAGE CREAM
CHEESE, SOFTENED

½ TEASPOON VANILLA EXTRACT

¼ TEASPOON RED OR GREEN
FOOD COLORING

1. Preheat the oven to 350° F. Grease and flour a 9 x 9-inch baking pan. Combine the butter and chocolate in a microwave-safe bowl and microwave on medium for 30-second intervals until melted and smooth, removing to stir in between each interval. Let cool for 5 minutes.

2. Combine 2 eggs and ¾ cup of the sugar in a mixing bowl and beat with an electric mixer on medium speed for 1 minute. Add chocolate-and-butter mixture, beat for 1 minute, and then add the flour and salt. Beat until just blended and then spread into the prepared pan.

3. In a separate bowl, combine the remaining egg and sugar, the cream cheese, vanilla, and food coloring. Beat with an electric mixer on medium speed until light and fluffy. Spread on top of batter and use a fork to stir the layers together. Place in the oven and bake for 35 minutes, until the top is springy to the touch. Remove, allow the brownies to cool in the pan, and then cut into bars.

CRUNCHY PEANUT BUTTER AND GOBLETS OF JAM THUMBPRINTS

¾ CUP LIGHT BROWN SUGAR, FIRMLY PACKED

½ CUP GANJA BUTTER (SEE RECIPE ON PAGE 8), SOFTENED

1 CUP SMOOTH PEANUT BUTTER (NOT HOMEMADE OR NATURAL)

1 LARGE EGG AT ROOM TEMPERATURE

½ TEASPOON VANILLA EXTRACT

1 TEASPOON BAKING SODA

⅛ TEASPOON SALT

1 CUP ALL-PURPOSE FLOUR

1 CUP ROASTED PEANUTS, MINCED

1½ CUPS SEEDLESS RASPBERRY JAM

1. Preheat the oven to 375° F and line two baking sheets. Combine the brown sugar, butter, and peanut butter in a mixing bowl and beat at low speed with an electric mixer to blend. Increase the speed to high and beat for 3 to 4 minutes, until light and fluffy. Add the egg, vanilla, baking soda, and salt and beat for 1 minute. Slowly add the flour and beat until a soft dough forms.

2. Remove the dough in tablespoon-sized portions and roll them into balls. Roll the balls in the chopped peanuts and place the balls on the baking sheets, 1½ inches apart. Use your index finger to make a large depression in the center of each ball. Place the cookies into the oven and bake for 10 to 12 minutes, until the edges are brown. Remove, let cool for 2 minutes, and then transfer to wire racks to cool completely.

3. While the cookies are cooling, place the raspberry jam in a saucepan and cook over medium heat. Bring to a boil, while stirring frequently, and cook until the jam has been reduced by a quarter. Spoon a teaspoon of the jam into each cookie and allow it to set.

ACAPULCO GOLD POLVORONES (MEXICAN WEDDING COOKIES)

1 CUP GANJA BUTTER (SEE RECIPE ON PAGE 8), SOFTENED

1¾ CUPS CONFECTIONERS' SUGAR

1 CUP CAKE FLOUR

1 CUP SELF-RISING FLOUR

1 CUP ALMONDS, BLANCHED AND MINCED

½ TEASPOON VANILLA EXTRACT

1. Preheat the oven to 350° F and line two baking sheets. Place the butter in a mixing bowl with 1¼ cups of the sugar and beat at medium speed with an electric mixer until light and fluffy. Add the flours, almonds, and vanilla and beat until just combined. The dough should be very stiff. Add a few drops of hot water, if necessary, to make it pliable.

2. Remove the dough in tablespoon-sized portions and roll these into balls. Place the balls 1 inch apart on the baking sheets and flatten them slightly with the bottom of a glass that has been dipped in flour. Place in oven and bake for 12 to 15 minutes, until lightly browned. Remove from oven.

3. Sift remaining sugar into a shallow bowl and use a spatula to transfer the cookies to the bowl. Coat the cookies with the sugar and then transfer them to wire racks to cool completely.

GANJA GRANOLA COOKIES

1 CUP GANJA BUTTER (SEE RECIPE ON PAGE 8), SOFTENED

1 CUP LIGHT BROWN SUGAR, FIRMLY PACKED

¾ CUP GRANULATED SUGAR

2 LARGE EGGS

1 TEASPOON VANILLA EXTRACT

¾ CUP ALL-PURPOSE FLOUR

½ CUP WHOLE WHEAT FLOUR

1 TEASPOON BAKING SODA

½ TEASPOON BAKING POWDER

½ TEASPOON CINNAMON

¼ TEASPOON SALT

2 CUPS OATS

½ CUP UNSWEETENED COCONUT FLAKES

2 CUPS TRAIL MIX, COARSELY CHOPPED

1. Preheat the oven to 350° F and line two baking sheets. Combine butter, brown sugar, and granulated sugar in a mixing bowl and beat at low speed with an electric mixer to blend. Increase the speed to high and beat for 3 to 4 minutes, until light and fluffy. Add eggs and vanilla, beat until combined, and then add the flours, baking soda, baking powder, cinnamon, and salt. Beat at low speed until combined and then stir the oats, coconut, and trail mix in by hand.

2. Drop tablespoon-sized portions of the dough onto the baking sheets, 1½ inches apart. Place in the oven and bake for 12 to 15 minutes, until browned. Remove from the oven, allow cookies to cool for 3 minutes, and then transfer to wire racks to cool completely.

CRACKED UP CHOCOLATE ALMOND CRINKLE COOKIES

⅔ CUP SLIVERED ALMONDS

2 TABLESPOONS GRANULATED SUGAR

6 OZ. BITTERSWEET CHOCOLATE, FINELY CHOPPED

¼ CUP WHOLE MILK

½ CUP GANJA BUTTER (SEE RECIPE ON PAGE 8)

1½ CUPS LIGHT BROWN SUGAR, PACKED

2 LARGE EGGS AT ROOM TEMPERATURE

½ TEASPOON ALMOND EXTRACT

2 TABLESPOONS UNSWEETENED COCOA POWDER

2 TEASPOONS BAKING POWDER

½ TEASPOON SALT

2¾ CUPS ALL-PURPOSE FLOUR

¾ CUP CONFECTIONERS' SUGAR

1. Preheat the oven to 350° F. Place the almonds on a baking sheet and toast for 5 to 7 minutes, until lightly browned. Remove from the oven and transfer to a food processor. Add the granulated sugar and pulse until the almonds are very fine. Set the mixture aside.

2. Combine the chocolate and milk in a microwave-safe bowl and microwave on medium for 45-second intervals until melted and smooth, removing to stir in between each interval.

3. Combine the butter and brown sugar in a mixing bowl and beat at low speed with an electric mixer to blend. Increase the speed to high and beat for 3 to 4 minutes, until light and fluffy. Add the eggs one at a time and beat until combined. Add the chocolate-and-milk mixture, almond extract, cocoa powder, baking powder, and salt and beat for 1 minute. Slowly add the flour and beat until a stiff dough forms. Stir in the almonds and place the dough in the refrigerator for at least 2 hours, until it is firm.

4. Preheat the oven to 350° F and line two baking sheets. Sift confectioners' sugar onto a sheet of waxed paper. Remove tablespoon-sized portions of the dough, roll them into balls, and roll each ball in the confectioners' sugar until well coated. Place the balls 2 inches apart on the baking sheets, place in oven, and bake for 14 to 16 minutes, until the cookies are crackling and the edges feel dry. Remove, let cool for 2 minutes, and then transfer to wire racks to cool completely.

POWDER-COVERED MOCHA BASH BALLS

2 TABLESPOONS
INSTANT COFFEE

2 TABLESPOONS BOILING WATER

½ CUP GANJA BUTTER (SEE
RECIPE ON PAGE 8), SOFTENED
AND CUT INTO SMALL PIECES

⅓ CUP GRANULATED SUGAR

1 LARGE EGG AT
ROOM TEMPERATURE

½ TEASPOON PURE
VANILLA EXTRACT

¼ CUP UNSWEETENED
COCOA POWDER

1⅓ CUPS ALL-PURPOSE FLOUR

PINCH OF SALT

1 CUP CONFECTIONERS' SUGAR

1. Preheat the oven to 350° F and grease two baking sheets or cover them with silicon baking mats. Combine coffee and water in a small bowl and stir until the coffee has dissolved. Set aside and let cool.

2. Combine the butter and granulated sugar in a mixing bowl and beat at medium speed with an electric mixer until light and fluffy. Add the egg and vanilla, beat until well combined, and then add the cocoa powder and the coffee. Beat well and scrape the sides of the bowl as necessary. Reduce the speed to low, add the flour and salt, and beat until just combined.

3. Form dough into balls and place them 1 inch apart on the baking sheets. Place in the oven and bake for 15 to 18 minutes, until firm. Remove the sheets from the oven.

4. Sift confectioners' sugar into a shallow bowl and use a spatula to transfer a few cookies at a time into the bowl. Roll the cookies in the sugar until well coated and then transfer them to wire racks to cool completely.

SUGAR WEED SPRITZ

1 CUP GANJA BUTTER (SEE RECIPE
ON PAGE 8), SOFTENED

⅔ CUP GRANULATED SUGAR

2 LARGE EGGS AT
ROOM TEMPERATURE

1 TEASPOON VANILLA EXTRACT

2½ CUPS ALL-PURPOSE FLOUR

¼ TEASPOON SALT

COLORED SUGARS

SMALL CANDIES

CANDIED CHERRIES

1. Combine the butter and sugar in a mixing bowl and beat at low speed with an electric mixer to blend. Increase the speed to high and beat for 3 to 4 minutes, until light and fluffy. Add eggs and vanilla, beat for 1 minute, and then slowly add the flour and salt. Beat until a soft dough forms. Divide the dough in half and wrap each half in plastic. Press dough into pancakes and then place the dough in the refrigerator for at least an hour and up to 2 days.

2. Preheat the oven to 350° F and line two baking sheets. Use a cookie press to press the dough onto the baking sheets, 1 inch apart. Decorate with the colored sugars, small candies, and candied cherries as desired. Place in the oven and bake for 12 to 15 minutes, until the edges are brown. Remove from the oven, let cool for 2 minutes, and then transfer the cookies to wire racks to cool completely.

BONGED UP BAKLAVA

3½ CUPS WALNUTS

2½ CUPS GRANULATED SUGAR

1 TEASPOON GROUND
CINNAMON

¼ TEASPOON GROUND CLOVES

1 (1 POUND) PACKAGE OF
PHYLLO SHEETS, THAWED

1½ CUPS GANJA BUTTER (SEE
RECIPE ON PAGE 8), MELTED

1½ CUPS WATER

½ CUP HONEY

½ LEMON, THINLY SLICED

1 (3-INCH) CINNAMON STICK

1. Preheat the oven to 350° F. Place the walnuts on a baking sheet, place the sheet in the oven, and toast for 5 to 7 minutes, until lightly browned. Remove the pan from the oven and place the walnuts, ½ cup of the sugar, cinnamon, and cloves in a food processor. Pulse until the mixture is very fine.

2. Increase the oven's temperature to 375° F and grease a 12 x 16-inch rimmed baking sheet. Place the phyllo sheets on a plate and cover with plastic wrap or a damp paper towel to keep them from drying out. Place 1 sheet of phyllo on the baking sheet and brush with the melted butter. Repeat with 7 more sheets of phyllo, and spread ⅓ of the walnut mixture on top. Place 4 more sheets of phyllo dough on top, brushing each with butter. Spread ⅓ of the walnut mixture on top, and then repeat. Top the last layer of walnut mixture with the remaining sheets of phyllo dough, brushing each one with butter. Trim the edges to make a neat rectangle.

3. Cut pastry into 2-inch squares or triangles, taking care not to cut through the bottom crust. Place in the oven and bake for 25 to 30 minutes, until the top layer of phyllo is brown.

4. While the pastry is cooking, combine the remaining sugar, water, honey, lemon, and cinnamon stick in a saucepan. Bring to a boil over medium heat, while stirring occasionally, reduce heat to low and simmer for 5 minutes. Strain syrup and keep hot while pastry finishes baking.

5. Remove the baking sheet from the oven and pour the hot syrup over the pastry. Place the pan on a wire rack, allow to cool to room temperature, and then cut through to the bottom crust.

WARSAW WOWIE
FRIED COOKIES

3 LARGE EGGS AT
ROOM TEMPERATURE

¼ CUP WHOLE MILK

¾ CUP GRANULATED SUGAR

½ CUP GANJA BUTTER
(SEE RECIPE ON PAGE 8)

1 TEASPOON BAKING SODA

1 TEASPOON VANILLA EXTRACT

½ TEASPOON SALT

½ TEASPOON FRESHLY
GROUND NUTMEG

3½ CUPS ALL-PURPOSE FLOUR

VEGETABLE OIL FOR FRYING

1 CUP CONFECTIONERS' SUGAR
FOR DUSTING

1. Combine the eggs, milk, granulated sugar, and butter in a mixing bowl and whisk until well combined. Whisk in the baking soda, vanilla, salt, and nutmeg, and then add the flour. Mix until a soft dough forms, cover the bowl tightly, and chill in the refrigerator for at least 1 hour and up to 3 days.

2. Dust a work surface and a rolling pin with flour. Roll out the dough to an even thickness of ¼ inch. Cut dough into 1-inch wide strips. Cut strips on a diagonal at 3-inch intervals to form diamond-shaped cookies.

3. Pour 1½ inches of oil in a deep Dutch oven or saucepan. Heat to 375° F and add the cookies a few at a time, using a slotted spoon to turn them as they brown. When cookies are browned all over, remove, set to drain on paper towels, and sprinkle with confectioners' sugar. Serve immediately.

KENTUCKY BLUE BOURBON BALLS

2 CUPS PECANS, CHOPPED

1 CUP GANJA BUTTER (SEE RECIPE
ON PAGE 8), SOFTENED

2 POUNDS CONFECTIONERS'
SUGAR

½ CUP INFUSED BOURBON
(SEE RECIPE ON PAGE 42)

½ TEASPOON SALT

½ POUND BITTERSWEET
CHOCOLATE, CHOPPED

1. Preheat the oven to 350° F. Place the pecans on a baking sheet and toast for 5 to 7 minutes, until lightly browned. Remove the nuts from the oven and set aside.

2. Combine the butter and 1 pound of the confectioners' sugar in a mixing bowl and beat at low speed with an electric mixer to blend. Increase the speed to high and beat for 3 to 4 minutes, until light and fluffy. Add the remaining sugar, infused bourbon, and salt and beat for 2 minutes. Stir in the pecans and then transfer the mixture to the refrigerator. Chill for 2 hours, or until firm.

3. Place the chocolate in a microwave-safe bowl and microwave on medium for 45-second intervals until melted and smooth, removing to stir in between each interval. Allow chocolate to cool to 105° F.

4. Line a baking sheet and form butter-and-bourbon mixture into tablespoon-sized balls. Drizzle the chocolate over the balls and then transfer the sheet to the refrigerator. Refrigerate for 45 minutes, until the chocolate hardens.

MARIJUANA-INFUSED ALCOHOL

¼ OZ. MARIJUANA

3 OZ. ALCOHOL

1. Use a mortar and pestle to grind the weed into a powder. Soak it overnight in water to remove any dirt.

2. Drain and place the powder in a small jar. Pour the alcohol over it, seal the jar, and hide it in a cool, dark place for 2 weeks. Shake the jar once a day.

3. After 2 weeks, strain the liquid through a coffee filter and press to remove as much liquid from the weed as possible. Store the infused liquid in the refrigerator until ready to use.

CHEEBA CHOCOLATE WALNUT FUDGE

1 CUP WALNUTS,
COARSELY CHOPPED

¾ POUND QUALITY BITTERSWEET
CHOCOLATE, CHOPPED

2 OZ. UNSWEETENED
CHOCOLATE, CHOPPED

½ CUP GANJA BUTTER
(SEE RECIPE ON PAGE 8)

2 CUPS GRANULATED SUGAR

1 CUP BHANG BOOSTER
(SEE RECIPE ON PAGE 44)

1 TEASPOON PURE
VANILLA EXTRACT

VEGETABLE OIL SPRAY

1. Preheat the oven to 350° F and line a 9 x 9-inch baking pan with heavy-duty aluminum foil so that the foil extends over the sides. Spray the foil with vegetable oil spray.

2. Place the walnuts on a baking sheet, place it in the oven, and toast the walnuts for 5 to 7 minutes, until lightly browned. Remove from the oven and set the nuts aside.

3. Place the chocolates and the butter in a mixing bowl and set aside. Combine the sugar and Bhang Booster in a deep saucepan and cook over medium heat until the sugar has dissolved and the mixture is boiling. Continue to cook, while stirring constantly, until the mixture reaches 236° F. Pour this mixture over the chocolates and butter in the mixing bowl. Whisk until smooth and then stir in the walnuts and the vanilla.

4. Spread the fudge in an even layer in the baking pan. Refrigerate for 1 to 2 hours, until the fudge is set. Use the foil to lift the fudge out of the pan. Cut into squares.

BHANG BOOSTER

Bhang is a popular pot paste in South Asia, but this variation is made with evaporated milk so that it can last a long time in the refrigerator. Since it is heated during the infusing cycle, it can be used cold in dishes and still deliver its desired buzz. The fat in regular evaporated milk allows all that wonderful THC *to find a home, so avoid any low-fat versions.*

1 (12 OZ.) CAN EVAPORATED MILK

1 OZ. MARIJUANA, PULVERIZED

1. Place the evaporated milk and the marijuana in a small saucepan. Bring to a simmer over medium heat and stir occasionally. Reduce the heat to low and simmer for 10 minutes.

2. Strain through a liquid coffee filter, pressing hard to get as much liquid out of the weed as possible. Store the liquid in the refrigerator.

ABOUT CIDER MILL PRESS BOOK PUBLISHERS

Good ideas ripen with time. From seed to harvest, Cider Mill Press brings fine reading, information, and entertainment together between the covers of its creatively crafted books. Our Cider Mill bears fruit twice a year, publishing a new crop of titles each spring and fall.

"Where Good Books Are Ready for Press"

Visit us online at
cidermillpress.com
or write to us at
PO Box 454
12 Spring St.
Kennebunkport, Maine 04046